animals

Copyright © 1995 Aladdin Books Ltd.

Produced by
Aladdin Books Ltd.
28 Percy Street
London W1P 0LD

Designed by
David West Children's Book Design
Consultant
Nikki Connor, Cert. Ed.
teacher specializing in early education

First published in the United States in 1995 by
Copper Beech Books
an imprint of
The Millbrook Press
2 Old New Milford Road
Brookfield, Connecticut 06804

Library of Congress Cataloging-in-Publication Data
West, David.
Animals / by David West ; illustrated by David West.
p. cm. -- (Words about...)
Summary: Describes some of the different animals that live
on the American plains, in the ice and snow, at the seashore,
in deserts, in the woods, and in other specific habitats.
ISBN 1-56294-163-1 (trade hc.) -- ISBN 1-56294-908-X (lib. bdg.)
1. Animals--Juvenile literature. (1. Animals.) I. Title. II. Series.
QL49.W47 1995
591--dc20
95-24061
CIP AC

Printed in Belgium
5 4 3 2 1

Words about
animals

David West

COPPER BEECH BOOKS
BROOKFIELD, CONNECTICUT

Grassland animals

trunk

mane

This cuddly lion has a black mane.

vulture

elephant

tusk

lion

A family of lions is called a pride.

gazelle

cheetah

Hippos love mud baths.

dung beetle

Cheetahs are the fastest animals on land.

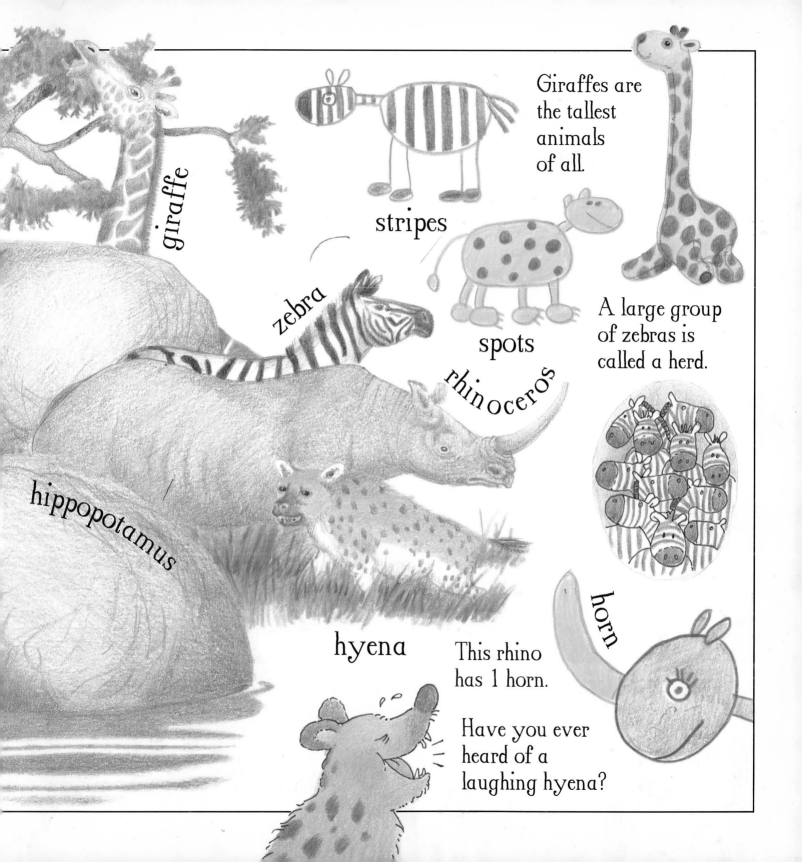

giraffe

stripes

Giraffes are the tallest animals of all.

spots

zebra

rhinoceros

A large group of zebras is called a herd.

hippopotamus

horn

hyena

This rhino has 1 horn.

Have you ever heard of a laughing hyena?

Prairie animals

Prairie chickens make a booming sound.

Coyotes like to howl at the moon.

Prairie dogs live together in towns.

rattle

Snakes have forked tongues.

Prairie dogs kiss each other when they meet.

bison

coyote

prairie chicken

prairie dogs

rattlesnake

eagle

Can you find
2 prairie dogs?

The bald eagle is the
symbol for the United
States. It isn't really
bald at all.

Kings used falcons
for hunting.

American badger

The bison has shaggy
brown fur.

falcon

whiskers

ears

jackrabbit

Animals of ice and snow

paw

walrus

penguin

puffin

narwhal

Walruses use
their sharp tusks
as ice picks.

Sometimes narwhals
fight with their tusks.

Penguins
cannot fly, but
they are great
swimmers.

The puffin has
3 fish in its
striped beak.

Snowshoe hares have big
feet to stop them from
sinking in the snow.

polar bear

reindeer

A polar bear's
white fur is perfect
camouflage.

hare

whale

A group of
whales is called
a pod.

seal

Jungle animals

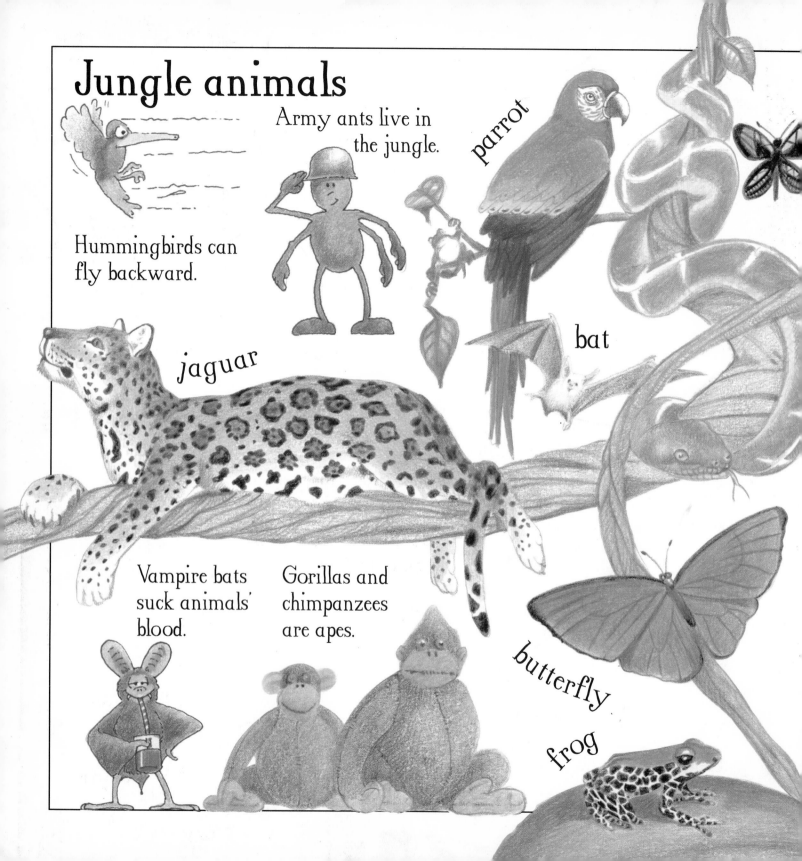

Hummingbirds can fly backward.

Army ants live in the jungle.

parrot

jaguar

bat

Vampire bats suck animals' blood.

Gorillas and chimpanzees are apes.

butterfly

frog

monkey

hummingbird

toucan

spider

sloth

gorilla

Monkeys use their tails for swinging through trees.

The toucan uses its beak as a nutcracker.

Which butterfly has bright blue wings?

There are 4 frogs in the picture. Can you find them all?

Snakes have scaly skin.

Seashore animals

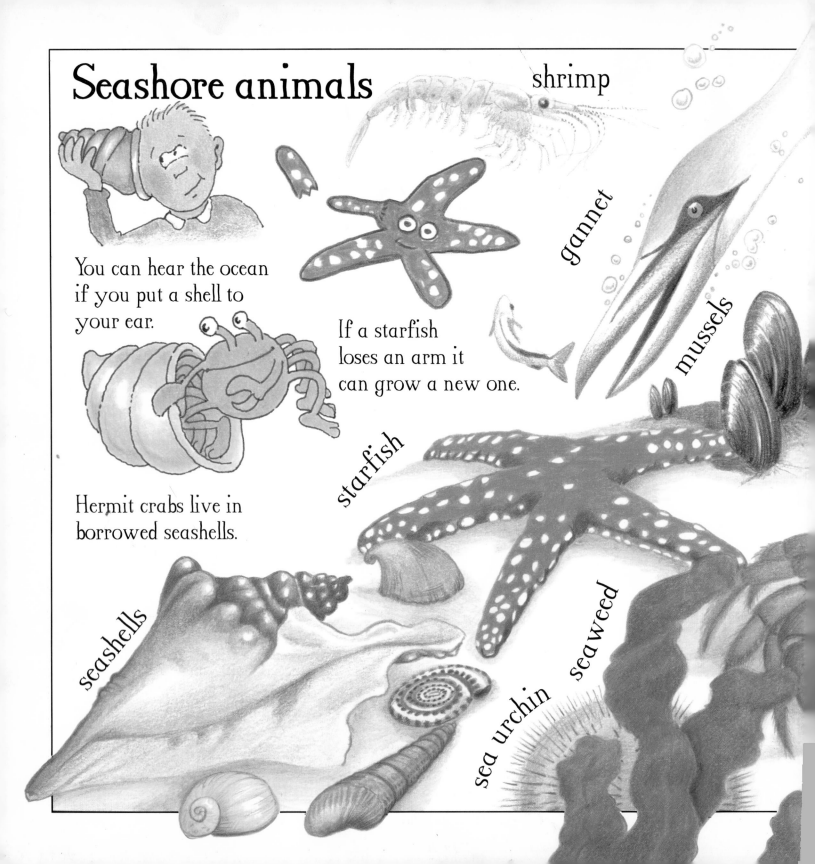

shrimp

You can hear the ocean if you put a shell to your ear.

If a starfish loses an arm it can grow a new one.

Hermit crabs live in borrowed seashells.

gannet

mussels

starfish

seashells

sea urchin

seaweed

How many arms does
a starfish have?

sea anemone

Did you know that
sponges are animals?

Seagulls have webbed
feet like ducks.

sea slug

The albatross is the biggest
seabird.

Lots of seashore
animals live in
rock pools.

crab

What color is
the seaweed?

Animals in the sea

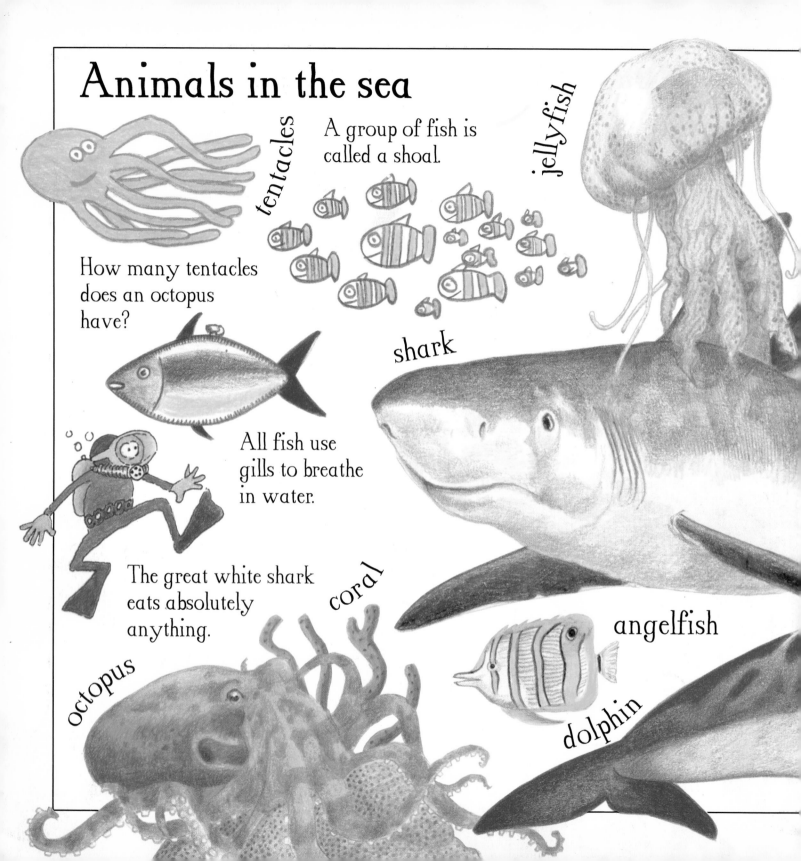

tentacles

A group of fish is called a shoal.

jellyfish

How many tentacles does an octopus have?

shark

All fish use gills to breathe in water.

The great white shark eats absolutely anything.

coral

angelfish

octopus

dolphin

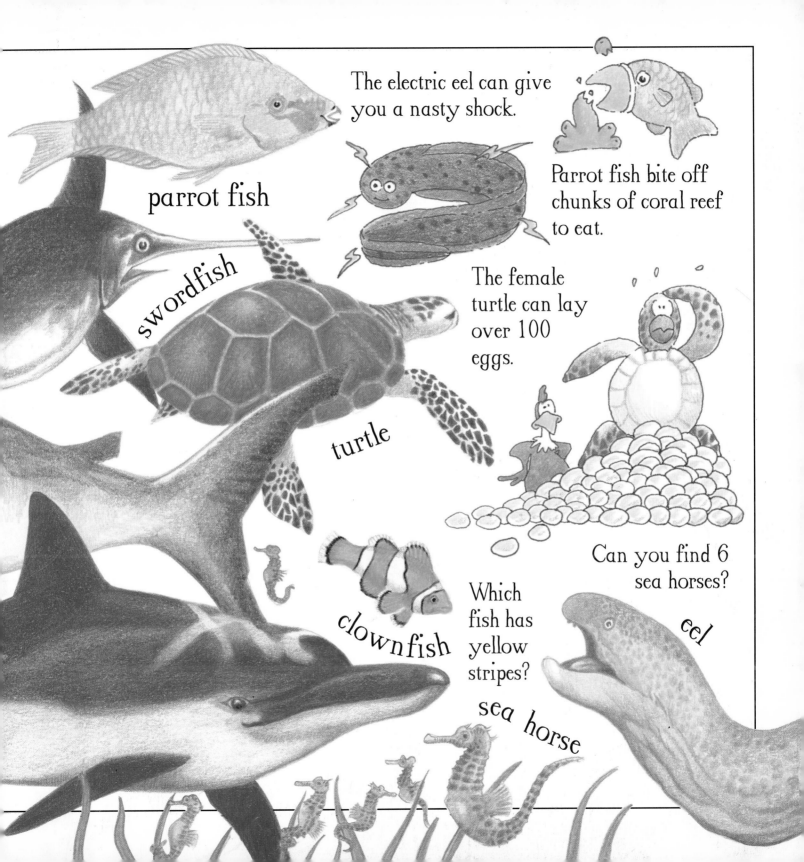

The electric eel can give you a nasty shock.

parrot fish

Parrot fish bite off chunks of coral reef to eat.

swordfish

The female turtle can lay over 100 eggs.

turtle

Can you find 6 sea horses?

clownfish

Which fish has yellow stripes?

eel

sea horse

Desert animals

A scorpion has a nasty sting in its tail.

Honeypot ants store nectar in their bodies.

Camels have two sets of eyelashes to keep the sand out of their eyes.

Ground squirrels use their tails as sunshades.

scorpion

A camel stores food in its hump.

jerboa

fox

owl

Some cacti are very prickly.

camel

Sandgrouse collect water in their feathers. Their chicks drink it.

sandgrouse

ant

The sun is orange in the evening.

lizard

There are 7 ants. Can you find them all?

tortoise

River animals

Flamingoes are pink.

swan

beak

Baby swans are called cygnets.

duck

The duckbill platypus digs for worms with its bill.

ducklings

pike

Crocodiles live in rivers and swamps.

newt

dragonfly

heron

toad

Some herons fish with feathers.

Beavers build dams in rivers.

A piranha has teeth as sharp as scissors.

The mother duck has 8 fluffy ducklings.

Eels are very slippery.

otter

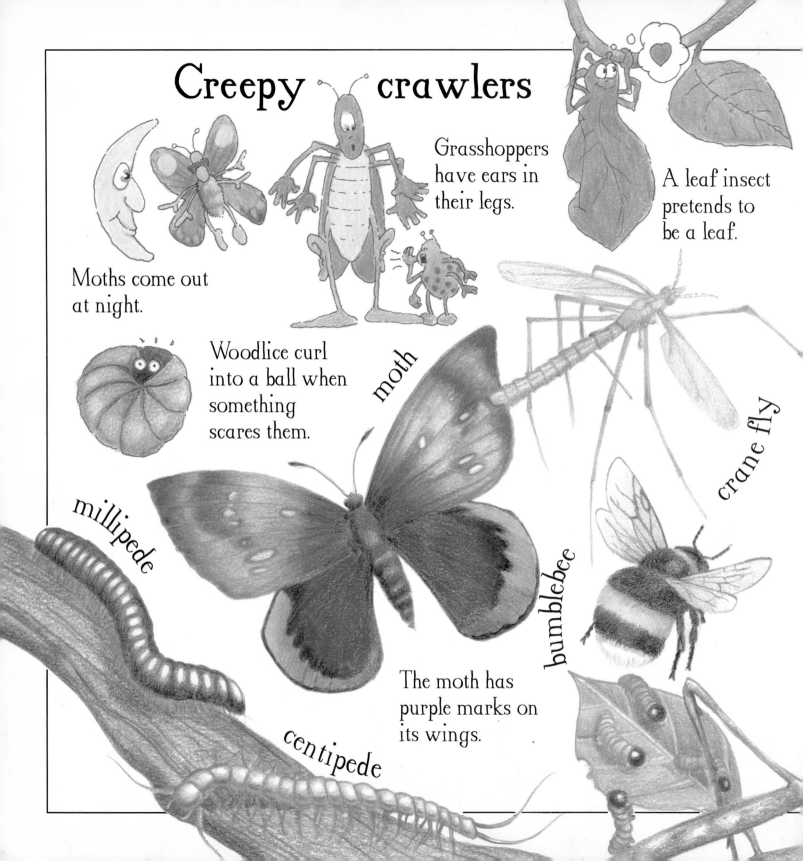

Creepy crawlers

Grasshoppers have ears in their legs.

A leaf insect pretends to be a leaf.

Moths come out at night.

Woodlice curl into a ball when something scares them.

millipede

moth

crane fly

bumblebee

centipede

The moth has purple marks on its wings.

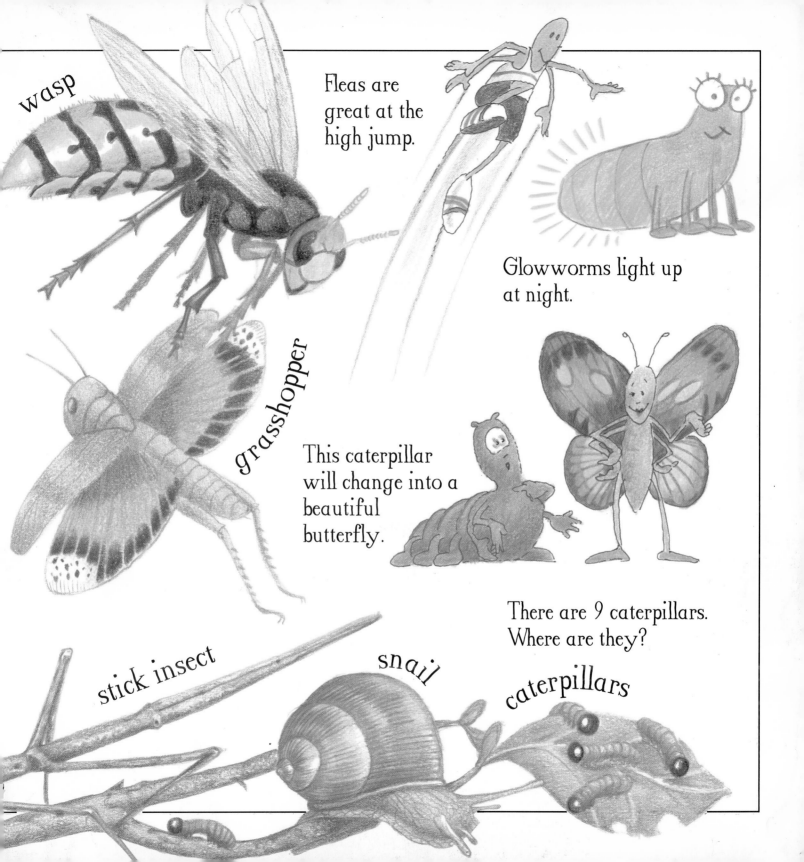

wasp

Fleas are great at the high jump.

Glowworms light up at night.

grasshopper

This caterpillar will change into a beautiful butterfly.

There are 9 caterpillars. Where are they?

stick insect

snail

caterpillars

Woodland animals

egg

nest

feather

A fox's bushy tail is called a brush.

Pandas eat bamboo.

pig

squirrel

The squirrel has hidden 10 acorns. How many can you find?

acorns

beetle

ladybug

woodpecker

deer

Oak trees grow from acorns.

antlers

rabbit

A baby koala rides on its mom's back.

fox

Which animal is red with black spots?

mouse

Bears love to eat honey.